Newborns, Nappies & No Sleep:
From Womb to Whaaa!
— A Hilarious Crash Course in Surviving Newborn Chaos

© 2025 Granny Dee Publishing
First Edition
Written by Granny Dee
(Granny Dee is the pen name of Donna Attard)

All rights reserved.
No part of this publication may be reproduced, stored in a retrieval system, or transmitted in any form or by any means — electronic, mechanical, photocopying, recording, or otherwise — without prior written permission from the publisher, except in the case of brief quotations used in reviews or articles.

This book is a work of humour, insight, and storytelling.
It is not intended as a substitute for professional medical, psychological, or parenting advice.
Please consult qualified professionals regarding the health of you or your child.

Publisher:
Granny Dee Publishing
PO Box 1129
Elanora 4221
Gold Coast, Australia

Website: hellogrannydee.com
Cover & Interior Design:
"By the ever-resourceful Granny Dee herself"

ISBN: 978-1-7635538-4-2

For every sleep-deprived, milky-shirted parent out there
— you're doing better than you think.

DEDICATION

To my sons,
You somehow survived my chaotic parenting, home haircuts, pritikin casseroles, a distinct lack of matching socks and my firm belief that duct tape could fix anything (even footy boots).
Now look at you:
grown men, raising kids
(& fur babies) of your own.
I am so happy and proud.

To the wonderful women who love my sons.....
You've seen the food feasts, the sock trails, the footy & fishing dramas - and you stayed. You're saints and...dare I say.. slightly crazy (like the rest of us). Thank you for loving my boys.

To my gorgeous grandchildren,
My tiny tornadoes of love - you remind me every day that life's sweetest chaos comes with hugs and giggles. I love you all more than words (and bliss balls) can say.

...and to all the exhausted, coffee-fuelled new parents out there -
May your coffee be strong, your baby's nap be longer than a sneeze and your shirt at least be the right way 'round by lunchtime. You now have the most wonderful, and hardest, job on earth. You're doing brilliantly! Keep going, loves. One day you'll sleep again....probably.

Introducing Granny Dee

Tucked away in a tiny off-grid eco-home, nestled in the bushland of Australia's Gold Coast, lives the wildly whimsical Granny Dee. With chooks clucking, kangaroos grazing, and kookaburras cackling in the trees, she's the barefoot matriarch of mischief and mayhem. Granny Dee's gathered a lifetime of tales, and knows a thing or two about living simply, and finding fun in the everyday.

Granny Dee's seen the world, danced through decades, raised a rascally tribe of kids and grandkids, and savours her chai tea every morning.

She's part earth mama, part laugh-out-loud sassy, and fully fabulous—wrapped in rainbow scarves, trailing the scent of eucalyptus and patchouli mystique wherever she roams.

Her books and card decks are stitched with laughter, Granny Dee wisdom, love, and the occasional chicken feather—so pull up a chair, pour yourself a hot cuppa, and prepare to be thoroughly grannified.

A Little Aussie Note from Granny Dee

WELCOME TO THE WORLD OF NAPPIES, DUMMIES & CUTE KOALAS

Hello, darlings! Before we dive headfirst into the wild, milky waters of newborn life, there's something you should know....

I'm proudly **Australian** - which means a few of the words in this book might sound a little different *(or downright confusing)* depending on where in the world you are.

So, just in case you're reading this from across the pond, or anywhere outside the land of kangaroos, prawns on the barbie and saying "G'day" — here's a quick translation of some of our favourite Aussie baby terms:

- Nappy = Diaper
- Dummy = Pacifier
- Singlet = Undershirt/vest
- Bathers = Swimmers - Aussie babies learn to swim early
- Cot = Crib
- Nappy Bag = Diaper Bag
- Baby Capsule = Infant car seat
- Biscuit/Bickie = Biscuit or cookie

No translation needed for love, cuddles and newborn chaos.

So pop the kettle on, grab a **Tim Tam** (a favourite Aussie bickie), and let's get into it.

Welcome to the Crazy World of Newborns

Or as Granny Dee calls it: "The Land of Crumbs, Cries and Cold Tea"

Hello darlings — if you've just entered the wild ride that is parenting,

Congratulations!

You now live in a world where sleep is mythical, (like unicorns), your house smells faintly of that missing wet nappy, and the mysterious stain on your jeans has been there for 3 days now.

But fear not, because this isn't your average parenting advice. Oh no — this is **Granny-style survival wisdom**, brewed strong like my chai tea and with just enough sass and fun to stay sane.

Newborn Survival Starter Pack

(besides sleep, hot coffee...and more sleep)

- **1 muslin cloth** ... or everything cloth: burp rag, tea towel, swaddle, superhero cape
- 3 hours of sleep in 12-minute chunks
- The ability to do everything one-handed
- At least one friend who won't judge you for crying over toast
- **Nappy cream** that's been used for 6 different things, none of which were the baby's bum

Granny Tip: And if you're wondering whether to shower or nap — always choose nap. No one's sniffing you but the baby, and they love you regardless.

A Smidge of
Newborn Myth-Busting

Myth 1: All newborns are sleepy, peaceful angels.

HA! Cute myth, but no. Be prepared for your tiny overlord to wail and wriggle at all hours.

Myth 2: Little babies love to stick to their sleep schedule.

Sure...until they decide to party at an ungodly hour...or have a 2 hour nap when you're waiting to go out.

Myth 3: Changing baby's nappy is always the same routine.

Bless your heart if you believe this, but you're in for some "interesting" surprises.

Myth 4: You'll instinctively know how to care for your newborn.

HA! No new parent has it perfect. Other than on Pinterest, of course.

Baby Myth #81

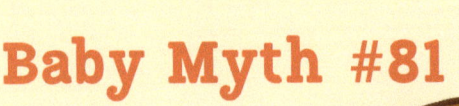

Your new baby will be bored if you don't entertain them.

Granny Dee:
Don't fret, darling. Show them the ceiling fan for the 37th time. They'll be mesmerised.

Spoiler Alert:
Oh love, your baby doesn't need a gadget that plays Mozart in three languages,
— they just need to be fed, snuggled, kept in a clean nappy
... and shown the ceiling fan now and then for a bit of top-tier entertainment.

Chapter 1
BRINGING BABY HOME

They Just Handed Us Our Baby

(With no training, no manual and a 'good luck' smile ....seriously, what are they thinking!!)

You did it! You survived childbirth. You are a legend....and now - jokingly - the birthing staff are letting you leave... with an actual human being who has zero regards for your personal space, sleep schedule or bladder control.

This is now getting real!

As you wobble out to the car, rather dishevelled and disoriented, clutching your tiny, slightly squishy bundle, a few realisations hit you square in the face:

- **Wait, they're not sending a professional with us?**
- **Are we even qualified to care for this small human?**
- **Whose idea was this??**

The First Car Ride: A True Test of Nerves

That first car ride home with baby is hands down the most stressful journey of your life. You will drive at the speed of a cautious turtle, while glaring at every car like a secret agent on a mission.

If a car passes you going 50km/hr in a 60 zone, you scream internally (coz you don't won't to upset the baby)
"THERE'S A NEW BABY IN THIS CAR!! DO YOU EVEN KNOW HOW TO DRIVE??"

Congratulations!
you're now officially parenting

The First Hour of Baby at Home

Minute 1
You place the baby in the fancy bassinet you spent 400 years picking out. Baby immediately screams like it's filled with hot volcanic lava.

Minute 6
Baby poops. Possibly in the bassinet. Possibly on you. Maybe both.

Minute 12
You basically wander through the house in a daze....turning in circles.

Minute 18
You question every decision you've ever made.

Minute 24
You try to eat a sandwich one-handed while cradling a red-faced, screaming gremlin ...wondering if the neighbours are already considering moving out due to 'baby noise'.

Minute 30
You Google "Can you actually break a baby by accident" and then cry again because Google says "no" but you're still not sure.

Minute 45
You accept that you will never sit down again. Standing is your new hobby. Baby is the boss.

Parenthood is a lot like trying
to assemble
IKEA furniture
while blindfolded.
You'll have no idea
what you're doing at first,
but eventually,
you'll figure it out.

Here's a Granny Dee secret:
No new parent knows what they're doing, especially in the beginning. The 'experts' (ie: parents, friends or Mr. Google) will give you a million different pieces of advice.
Just remember:
It's okay to listen, but trust your gut.
No one knows your baby like you do.

CHAPTER 2
I Googled 'Can You Die From Sleep Deprivation?'

(Spoiler: You can't. Just hang in there)

The Honest Truth About Newborn Sleep

Babies don't 'sleep.'

They nap aggressively for 7 minutes at a time, just long enough for you to start a load of laundry, reheat a sad cup of coffee or fall into a pit of false hope.

SLEEPS LIKE A BABY...

(WHICH MEANS NOT AT ALL)

SLEEP MODE

Sleep is a theoretical concept that babies flirt with but rarely commit to.

If your baby activates Sleep Mode:

- Remain completely still.
- Do not sneeze, breathe loudly or think aggressive thoughts.

If Sleep Mode fails, place baby in a carrier, walk in figure-eight pattern, and chant,

"The universe is vast, and sleep is but a distant dream."

You've been rocking, feeding, patting, and pacing for five hours—then Grandma walks in, says one word, and the baby's snoring like a pensioner after Christmas lunch. Don't worry, love—it's not you. All babies save their loudest drama for Mum, and you're still doing an amazing job.

Tale from a
SLEEP-DEPRIVED 'MUM' BRAIN

I've been wearing maternity clothes for so long now, I decide it's high time for a post-baby outfit. New clothes will make me feel human again, right?

In theory. I head into the shop, briefly marvel at my non-pregnant shape in the fitting room mirror, and select a new top to buy.

In reality. I start to head out of the shop… only to remember that I've left the baby in the pram by the changing rooms.

"Darling, that's not a fail. That's *mum brain* - a very real, very temporary, and often funny side-effect of sleep deprivation, leaky boobs and sheer survival mode. Trust me, it passes, eventually." *Granny Dee xx*

Ah, sleep. Remember sleep?

That soft, dreamy thing you used to luxuriate in before your tiny overlord arrived?

Yeah, forget it. It's gone now.

You've entered the Wild West, darling, and the sheriff here is an 8-pound dictator with the sleep schedule of a caffeinated raccoon.

Let's bust the biggest myth of parenthood right now:

"Sleeping like a baby" actually means "baby waking up every 17 minutes, screaming like they've been shot out of a cannon."

Signs You're A Sleep-Deprived Parent

You put the car keys in the fridge.

You thanked the toaster for its service.

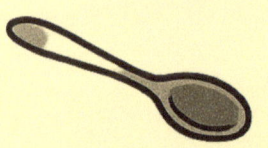
You cried because you dropped a spoon

You tried to change the TV channel with your phone

You forgot the name of your own dog/cat

The question so many sleep-deprived parents have asked at 2am

Why do baby clothes have so so many snaps?

CHAPTER 3
NAPPIES, POOP EXPLOSIONS AND THE MYTH OF THE 'QUICK CHANGE'

Oh, love — buckle up. Granny Dee has seen some things... and most of them required wipes, wine, and waterproof flooring.

How Many Nappy Changes Does a Newborn Need?

Short answer: About 10–12 a day.
Real answer: Enough to make you question every life decision that led to this moment.

Granny Dee's Nappy Change Math

- 1 wee = 1 nappy
- 1 poo = 1 nappy (if you've mastered the nappy change routine - otherwise up to 3 nappies & dozens of wipes)
- 1 phantom poo (false alarm) = still 1 nappy, your soul, and your last nerve
- 1 blowout = new nappy, new outfit, new will to live
- Nighttime nappies = a fun game called *"How asleep is too asleep to change them?"*

Granny Dee's Truth Bombs

- It'll be time for a nappy change every time you actually sit down with a hot drink.
- The one time you don't pack spare nappies (or outfits) = code brown explosion at the local café.
- Nappy bin smell? That's eau de parenthood.

Mantra for the Overwhelmed

"It's not forever. It just feels like it at 3am."

Granny Dee's Guide to Changing a Newborn's Nappy

Because cleaning tiny bums requires wipes, wit and a will of steel.

Step 1: Prepare Your Battle Station

Right then, soldier. Before you even think about removing baby's nappy, gather your gear like you're heading into battle — because, well, you are.

You'll need:
- One clean nappy
- Approximately 6–15 wipes (triple that if baby's done a poo explosion - or you're still trying to master this nappy change battle)
- A change mat or an old towel that's seen things
- A clean outfit (for baby... or you... or both)
- A cup of tea slowly going cold nearby (you won't drink it, but it makes you feel civilised)

Granny Dee Tip:

Maintain eye-to-eye contact with baby at all times during nappy change. Never, ever utter the words, "I'll just grab the wipes." (& break eye contact) That's exactly how the Poop Trail of '98 started, and we still don't speak of it.

Step 2: Position Baby
Lay your little one gently on the change mat.
Smile sweetly and say something soothing, like:
"Alright, my tiny darling — what fresh horror have you got for me today?"

(Bonus points if you maintain eye contact like you're in a Western standoff.)

Step 3: The Great Reveal
Undo the tabs or clips.
Breathe deeply - or not, depending on the smell.
Lift with caution
— and for heaven's sake, brace yourself.

Now, peek inside like you're opening Tutankhamun's tomb with nothing but hope and hand sanitiser.

What you might find:
- A mild mustard dollop
- A gentle, earthy smear that says "just a practice go"
- Or...the dreaded poonami — a full-scale explosion that defies gravity, physics, and human dignity

Common sub-step:
Baby pees mid-change. You gasp. They giggle. A fine mist arcs gracefully across the change table. Panic ensues.
You scramble for anything — clean nappy, burp cloth, sock — and attempt to shield the blast with nothing but trembling hands and fading hope.

Step 5: New Nappy, Fresh Hope
Slide clean nappy under baby's bum like a seasoned ninja.
Tabs snug but not tight
— you're not strapping them to a rocket.
Ensure ruffles are out to prevent "side seepage."

Step 6: Celebrate (Quietly)
Zip up, button down, or snap the snaps (incorrectly, twice).

Give baby a kiss. Sniff to confirm your work. Then wash your hands and ask the universe: *"How can someone so small create so much chaos?"*

Granny Dee Tip:
**Don't forget to smile
at your success.
You've earned it.**

Final Thought from Granny Dee
- You will forget to pack nappies exactly once — and never again.
- You will laugh............Eventually.

And remember:
"It's just a nappy.
It's not a personality test.
You're doing fine."

"Changing nappies

is just like life, darling

— messy, unpredictable,

occasionally explosive...

but somehow,

still wrapped in love"

— Granny Dee x

How Deep is Your Poop Knowledge?
There are no winners here. Just survivors.

1. What is a "Poonami"?
A) That curry you foolishly ordered extra hot
B) Pre-disaster, false alarm nappy warning
C) The reason you sobbed in Woolies car park
D) A Code Brown catastrophe sent from the bowels of the earth.

Granny Dee says:
"If you chose anything other than D, you've clearly never had to remove a beyond-repair, poonami-damaged onesie."

2. You forgot to put a clean nappy under baby before taking the dirty one off. What happens next?
A) Nothing, you're lucky
B) Baby pees in your eye
C) The couch is never the same again
D) All of the above

3. How many wipes does it take to clean one newborn poop?
A) 1–2
B) 3–5
C) 6–12
D) The limit does not exist

4. What's the best way to tell if a nappy is "full"?
A) Sniff test
B) Squish test (not recommended)
C) When it starts to sag like a full fruit hammock
D) You'll know. Oh, you'll know.

5. What is a "quick change"?
A) A lie
B) A rare and mythical event, spoken of in hushed tones
C) A risky game of speed vs splash
D) Something only grandparents pretend to believe in

6. Why do babies always choose to poop just after a fresh nappy goes on?
A) Cosmic timing
B) Revenge
C) To keep you humble
D) All of the above

7. You've just changed baby's nappy. You turn around. What's missing?

A) The wipes
B) Your sanity
C) The baby
D) All three

8. How do you respond to a "code brown" that has leaked up to the shoulder blades?

A) Cry
B) Hose everything down
C) Deep breath, big sigh, then begin the cleanup.
D) Call Granny Dee

9. What's the most important skill for nappy changing?

A) One-handed precision
B) Jedi reflexes
C) The ability to laugh while being peed on
D) All of the above

Your Score:

Give yourself 1 biscuit for each C or D answer.

If you scored over 6 biscuits, **congratulations** — you're officially qualified to lead:

Special Ops: Nappy Division.

SPECIAL OPS: NAPPY DIVISION

CHAPTER 4
MILK BAR
(OPEN ALL DAY & NIGHT)

Granny Dee on Feeding a Newborn
A tale of boobs, bottles, burps and questionable smells.

Step 1: Accept That You're a 24-Hour Café Now
Whether you're breastfeeding, bottle feeding, or some glorious chaotic combo of both, just know:
- You're the barista, the chef and the kitchen hand now
- The customer is always hungry
- ...and sometimes screams at your service

Step 2: It's Called Cluster Feeding Because You'll Cluster Cry Too
Those "feed every 2–3 hours" instructions? They forgot to mention it's from the start of the feed — not the end.
Which means:
Feed. Burp. Nappy. Cuddle. Cry. Snooze. Repeat.

Step 3: Latch, Reject, Snooze, Repeat..endlessly
Newborns will:
- Latch beautifully one minute
- Reject you like a bad Tik Tok reel the next time
- Fall asleep mid-feed
- Then wake up as soon as you sit down with toast and a hot drink

Step 4: Burp Baby Like You Mean It
A burp is not optional.
It's preventative maintenance.
Skip it, and you're risking a milk volcano across your shoulder.
Bonus points if baby throws up after you've changed into clean clothes. Classic.

Step 5: The Internet Has 4,202 Opinions on Feeding
And you know what? None of them live in your house at 2am.
Fed is best.
Fed is fine.
Fed while crying and holding your boob like a squished balloon? Still counts.

Granny's Feeding Survival Mantras:
- "It's not forever, even if it feels like a looped sitcom called 'Guess Who's Hungry Again.'"
- "Your baby is not rating your performance. That's what future teenagers are for."
- "Feeding is bonding, even if it's damp, leaky, and a bit shouty."

FUELING INSTRUCTIONS

Babies require 98% of their body weight in breastmilk, formula, or spiritual sustentance daily.

Crying is often a sign of low fuel, though it could also be due to:
- ★ A cosmic misalignment
- ★ A scratchy sock
- ★ or the sudden realisation that their left toe is attached to their body forever.

When in doubt: feed, cuddle, and chant "You are the light of my life" softly into their hair.

Granny says:

"I chuckle every time I hear a new parent say, 'The baby will fit into our routine.' Darling, that baby's about to reschedule your entire existence—including your toilet breaks."

ZERO TEETH, UNLIMITED POWER

CHAPTER 5
Why Is the Head Hole So Small?!

Granny Dee's Guide to Dressing a Newborn

Step 1: Choose an outfit

Congratulations. You've just entered the 'Newborn Clothing Mystery'.

- Lots of clothes, and yet nothing clean
- Some outfits are too hot
- Some are too cold
- And some that look like they were designed by a committee of drunk elves who have never seen a baby

Granny tip #1: If it has 19 snaps, throw it in the bin and start over. You don't need that kind of stress in your life.

Granny tip #2: Don't get too attached to what your baby wears. Chances are they'll poop in it in under three minutes. Probably twice.

Step 2: Prepare the baby (and yourself)

Lay them down gently. Smile lovingly.
They will immediately go full ferret: arms flailing, knees to chest, head flopping like a marionette in a windstorm.

Granny Tip: Speak calmly. Sing a song. Cry a little. And remember — the outfit was cute, but nudity is always an option.

Step 3: Battle the head hole
It looks like it should fit.
But somehow this hole — designed for newborns — seems smaller than your thumb ring. Try to stretch it gently. Try not to panic. Try not to mutter ancient curses under your breath.

Granny Tip: If you're wondering whether the head hole shrank in the wash or your baby suddenly grew a melon-sized head overnight — the answer is yes.
Just breathe, stretch gently....and keep going.

Step 4: Socks
You will:
- Lose them
- Find them in the nappy bag
- Lose them again
- Consider taping them on

Granny Tip: Accept that babies don't wear socks — they're not worth the stress!

Step 5: Final Check
- Outfit on
- Zip zipped
- Baby vaguely resembles a potato in a beanie
- You? Exhausted. But proud.

Step 6: Accept Your Fate (and Keep the Nappy Bag Packed)

So, the outfit is on, the baby looks semi-presentable, and you're teetering on the edge of emotional collapse.

Naturally, you think:
"We'll just pop out for a bit."
Darling... don't.

But if you must, take this wisdom:
- Always pack three spare outfits (minimum) — one for baby, one for you, and one for whatever poor soul is holding them when disaster strikes
- Wet wipes are non-negotiable
- Bibs? Optional. Full body hazmat suit? Ideal

Granny Tip: Lower the bar. If everyone makes it home fed, semi-dressed, and only mildly traumatised, you're not just surviving — you're winning.

Granny Says:

'If you're not sweating and apologising trying to dress the baby... you're doing it wrong'

Granny Dee's Parting Words

"They don't care what they wear.
They care that you love them.
So if today's fashion is
'onesie with milk stain
and unmatched mittens,'
you're winning."

THE ONESIE OLYMPICS

Getting your wriggly, red-faced newborn into a onesie is like dressing an octopus

Bonus points if there are snaps instead of a zipper.
You will always get at least one snap mismatched.

Domestic Goddess? Please. I'm Just Trying to Find the Dry and Clean Onesie.

When they handed you your baby in that soft hospital blanket, they forgot to mention one very important thing:

Warning: This model leaks, spits, and self-destructs outfits hourly.

By Day Three at home, the house has already begun to disappear beneath a creeping tide of muslin cloths, baby onesies, bibs, and whatever that mystery item was that might have been a towel, once, before 'The Baby Has Arrived' moment.

You start off optimistic.
You sort whites and colours. You even fold the tiny socks into little smiley bundles.

By Day Six, you're dumping everything into the machine like a possum hyped up on energy drinks and whispering,
"Am I secretly doing laundry for another family? A small village? Half the continent?!"

You ask yourself questions like:
- "How can one tiny bum produce 47 outfits in 24 hours?"
- "Is that milk, spit-up, or some other mystery stain?"
- "Did I just wash the remote again?"

The baby, of course, is unfazed.
They look directly into your soul, unleash another suspicious dribble, and fall asleep like a soap opera villain, mid-plot.

Eventually, your entire wardrobe becomes:
- One pair of leggings (now crunchy)
- A top that smells faintly of curdled dairy
- And a burp cloth tucked fashionably over your shoulder at all times

(Bonus points if you wear it to bed, just in case.)

And just when you think you've washed the last thing? The baby throws up onto a fresh onesie. You cry. They smile. You accept your fate.

LAUNDRY ISN'T A CHORE ANYMORE - IT'S A LIFESTYLE. EMBRACE IT. NAME YOUR WASHING MACHINE. SEND GRATITUDE CARDS TO THE SPIN CYCLE. AND ALWAYS CHECK THE MACHINE AT THE END OF THE WASH FOR THAT ONE ROGUE SOCK.

CHAPTER 6
HOW'S THE FIRST WEEK GOING, LOVE?

The Myth and The Mayhem

Oh, love... the first week home with a newborn is like being thrown into a sleep-deprived reality show with no script, no clues, and a cast of one - one leaky, screaming human.

Day One: You're Home... Holy Moly?
You leave the hospital with a fragile little bundle and the staff smiling like,
"Good luck, sweetheart. Hope you read the fine print!"
You open your front door like you're smuggling a Fabergé egg into a dance party.
And then it hits you: **there are no nurses here. No call buttons.** Just you... and 'The Baby'.

Day Two: The Nappy Has Turned Against You
You've changed 14 nappies in 12 hours. You've Googled "how to remove poo from cat hair."
You say "I've got this" out loud, then sob into a wipe that, you think, was already used.

Day Three: Feeding, Crying, Feeding, Crying (You Too)

You're up every 42 minutes. Baby is cluster feeding.

You've developed a sixth sense for whether a cry means "feed me," "burp me," or "I just enjoy watching you unravel."

Day Four: The Paranoia Sets In

You stare at the baby while they sleep.
Are they breathing?
Are they too quiet?
TOO QUIET???!
You lean in.
They snort.
You flinch.
You do this 67 times.

Day Five: You're Not Sure What Day It Is

Your hair is 60% dry shampoo.
You said "nappy cream" instead of "mayonnaise" in a conversation with your partner.
You found the TV remote in the fridge and calmly accepted it as your new normal.

Day Six: Laundry, Laundry, Panic, Laundry

You've washed 19 onesies, 11 burp cloths, and a towel you didn't even know you owned.
Everything smells faintly of sour milk and desperation.

Day Seven: You Made It, Darling
You're still standing (just).
The baby smiled (maybe it was wind, but who cares).
You're wearing actual pants.

You've earned your badge:
Survivor: Newborn Island.

Granny Dee's Advice for Week One:
- You will cry in the laundry basket. That's normal.
- You can't spoil a baby with cuddles. Only with disco lights and battery-operated swing chairs.
- You are doing enough — even if that's just keeping the tiny human alive while eating toast over the sink.

Granny Dee says:
"The first week is chaos with a side of cuddles. You'll forget half of it — the time, the tears, even where you left your tea... but you'll never forget that overwhelming, dizzying love you didn't know you were capable of. The kind that changes everything — even on three hours of sleep and unwashed hair."

Your baby is tougher...
and smarter than you realise.
Prepare to be outmanoeuvred
constantly by this little person
who can't even hold their own
head up yet. Your life will
never... and I mean *never*...
be the same.
In a mostly
good way.

A Fun, Totally Unscientific Quiz on Newborn Mayhem

1. How many hours of sleep did you get last night?
A. What is sleep?
B. 3 hours... in 17-minute intervals
C. Slept standing up during a 3am feed
D. I blinked rapidly — does that count?

2. Your baby starts crying. What do you do first?
A. Panic and Google "newborn crying again.....HELP"
B. Offer a boob or bottle....again
C. Sniff the nappy like a wine buff
D. Cry with them — solidarity!

3. Where's the dummy/pacifier?
A. Lost to the sock dimension
B. In the dog's mouth
C. Under your thigh, surprise!
D. Attached to your bra strap with a safety pin

4. How many cups of tea/coffee have you made...and NOT drunk?
A. 5 and counting
B. The kettle's on for the 14th time
C. Cold tea is my love language
D. I chew the coffee beans straight now, it's easier

5. What did you last find in your hair?
A. Baby puke
B. My missing biscuit from two days ago
C. A dummy
D. No idea but it's sticky!

6. When did you last shower?
A. Does going over the body with baby wipes count?
B. I washed my hands — close enough
C. Can't remember........
D. Yesterday! (Because grandma came over!)

7. What's on your shirt right now?
A. Mystery stain #8
B. Leaked milk and pride
C. Tears. Not sure whose.
D. Toast that somehow fused itself on

8. Your partner asks if you want anything from the shops. You say:
A. Wine, chocolate, nappies (in that order)
B. "A time machine, thanks."
C. "Just go. Please. Go."
D. "Surprise me with a treat for us both"

9. Most repeated phrase of the week?
A. "Is this normal?"
B. "Why are YOU crying?"
C. "Quick! Where's the wipes?"
D. "I love you baby, but please sleep."

10. Do you feel like you've got this?
A. No, but I have snacks
B. Somewhat... in a 'winging it with wet hair' kind of way
C. Ask me after another coffee
D. Heck yes...mostly...sort of.

Quiz Answers

Mostly A's
You're hanging on by a thread. It's okay, love. It gets funnier. Ish.

Mostly B's
You're flying by the seat of your post-pregnancy leggings, and I respect that.

Mostly C's
You're sipping cold tea and dry toast like a warrior. You've got this, legend.

Mostly D's
You're thriving in the chaos! Or at least pretending to.

Whatever letter you got, darling
— A, B, C, or D
— you deserve a medal and a nap.
Probably in that order.

This newborn gig is messy, magical, mildly ridiculous, and full of moments that will make you laugh (eventually).

CHAPTER 7
Granny's No-Fluff Survival Guide
These Worked in '81 and I'm Still Here, Aren't I?

Granny Dee Approved Parenting Hacks for Newborns

Sleep When Baby Sleeps, or Don't
Forget the pressure to nap. Use that quiet time for whatever keeps you sane: a cuppa, a cry, or watching trash TV.

Silent Ninja Nappy Change
Prep like a ninja before the change. Wipes open. Nappy ready. Distraction in place. It's a stealth mission.

The Doorbell Takedown
Stick a sign on your door - "Baby sleeping. Disturb at your own peril!"

Night Feeds = Snack Time for Mum Too
Keep a little "mum stash" of snacks by the feeding chair. Almonds, fruit, chocolate, whatever gets you through.

Blame Mercury Retrograde
When baby's unsettled, nothing is working, and you've ruled out everything-blame it on the planets.

♥ **Final Granny Dee Truth:**
Parenting isn't about being perfect. It's about showing up — with love and lots of wipes.
**The baby's still surviving?
You're doing better than you think.**

FORGET THE HIGH-TECH GADGETS
THESE ARE THE TRUE PARENTING ESSENTIALS

TWO HANDS & A FORGIVING HEART

One for holding the baby. One for catching vomit. A forgiving heart for when you forget which hand did which.

WIPES, WIPES, MORE WIPES

Reusable? Brilliant. Disposable? No judgement. Just have them everywhere. In the car. Down your shirt. Under your pillow. In your dreams. (or do as I used to do and use damp face cloths or a cloth nappy)

A HOT DRINK THAT WILL REPEATEDLY GO COLD

Could be herbal tea. Could be coffee. Could be an oat-milk turmeric mushroom latte. Doesn't matter. It's more about hope than hydration

PACE (LIKE A SLOW SLOTH)

Lower your bar of expectations. Then lower it again. If your child is loved, fed (ish), and relatively dry, you're winning. Perfection is for Pinterest. *You're parenting in the wild.*

GRANDMA (OR SPECIAL FRIEND) MAGIC

The gentle voice that says, "It's okay." The eyes that've seen it all and still smile. The heart that loves without conditions, and the hands that hold space—not just babies. If you've got a real grandma (or special friend) nearby, you're lucky. If not—be your own damn wise woman or man.

You've got this.

Granny Dee Says

No one is nailing parenting. At best, newborn parents are duct-taping it together and hoping it holds until bedtime.

At worst, you're googling 'Is it okay to play white noise for 10 hours straight?'

(Answer: Yes. Set it to 'Underwater Bliss' and pretend you're a mermaid escaping to a place where laundry doesn't exist.)

Celebrate the victories - like showering two days in a row - and laugh at the rest.

You'll know you're a parent when a solo trip to the supermarket feels like a holiday.

GRANDMA'S CORNER

1. If the baby is loud, give milk.

2. Don't fret over weird poop. Trust me—I've seen it all.

3. Swaddle, sway, and whisper: "Please go to sleep!"

4. Hold the baby, hold the baby, then hold the baby some more.

CHAPTER 8
CUP OF TEA, DEEP BREATH, YOU'VE GOT THIS

Granny Dee's Parting Pearls of Wisdom

Darling, the laundry can wait.
The dishes can pile up.
The house can look like a soft toy explosion — it doesn't matter.

What matters is this moment — when your baby finally surrenders to sleep, their tiny chest rising against yours, that sweet snuffly snore tickling your collarbone.

Breathe it in.
Soak up the weight of that little body melted into yours —
because nothing in this world is closer to pure, honest love.

Yes, the chaos will return. It always does.
But these precious, quiet in-between moments?
They're gold.

And one day — sooner than you think — they'll be a sulky teenager raiding your fridge and rolling their eyes so hard it's audible.
But that's a whole other chapter... and yes, I've got a book coming for that too.

The Magic and Madness of Newborn Parenting

"Oh, it's a ride, alright – equal parts cuddles, chaos, and questionable smells. One minute you're gazing at your baby like they're made of stardust, the next you're Googling 'is it normal to cry over spilled breast milk?' But you'll never laugh, cry, or love harder in your life. And that, sweetheart, is the joy of it all."

WHAT THEY SAID VS WHAT REALLY HAPPENS
(aka: Lies They Told With A Straight Face)

"Babies are bundles of joy"
And explosive body functions

"Trust your instincts"
My instinct just Googled 'why is baby grunting like a goat?

"You'll love every minute!"
I loved the five minutes of peace. They were nice

"Cherish these precious moments"
I'm cherishing the moment I got 3 hours of uninterrupted sleep

"Sleep when baby sleeps!"
And cook when baby cooks, right?

"Breastfeeding is a beautiful bond"
It's a latch-on-latch-off-latch-on milk fight club

"You'll" glow!
It's sweat & tears....& more tears

Well, you've made it to the end — in one piece hopefully, mostly dressed, and only mildly covered in something suspicious.

I'm proud of you. Truly.

Remember: there's no such thing as a perfect parent.

Only the kind of parents who love fiercely, try their best, make lots of mistakes, laugh through the chaos... and know exactly when it's time to hide in the pantry with a biscuit.

You've got this. And when you don't... that's what I'm here for.

Now go put the kettle on, darling. You've earned it.
Sending huge hugs, Granny Dee xx

Stay Connected, Darling

Because the giggles
(and glorious chaos) don't stop here.
Loved the book?
Craving more cheeky chuckles, biscuit-fuelled wisdom, and light-hearted takes on life's wild moments and wonky milestones?
I've got you.
Let's laugh our way through life
— one eye-roll and teacup at a time.

Find Granny Dee Online:

Website
hellogrannydee.com
Sage advice with a giggle-laugh on the side.

Social Media
IG: @hello.granny.dee
Behind-the-scenes silliness, parenting truths, eco hacks, and a chook named Gladys.

Granny Dee 'Parenting Collection'
(available now or coming soon)

Bottles, Boobs and Bedlam
Surviving Baby's First Year

Parenting: Cuddles, Chaos & Grandma Clues
How to Keep Your Kids Alive & Your Sanity Intact.....(Mostly!)

Granny Dee's Guide to Sibling Jealousy
So, the New Baby is Home....and the Toddler's Definitely Not Impressed!

Preggasaurus Rex
Granny Dee's Tips on Surviving Pregnancy Without Losing Your Mind

Toxic Teddies & Dodgy Ducks
Granny Dee spills the beans on the hidden toxins in baby toys - and how to keep your baby safe from these dangers.

Granny Dee Cleans House
Eco Friendly and Non Toxic Home Cleaning Recipes, all with a side of Granny Dee sass.

www.ingramcontent.com/pod-product-compliance
Lightning Source LLC
Chambersburg PA
CBHW041306110426
42743CB00037B/14